Keep Kissing

Keep Kissing

A Simple Little Book About Love and Marriage

Rand H. Packer

© 2010 Rand H. Packer

All Rights Reserved.

ISBN 13: 978-0-615-38840-3
e. 1

Published by: Spouse Spice LLC

Cover design by Amanda D. Beck
Cover design © Spouse Spice LLC

Printed in the United States of America
10 9 8 7 6 5 4 3 2 1
Printed on acid-free paper

To all husbands and wives, who, through warm and winter keep trying to learn and love in this wondrous world we call **wedlock**. There is a reason a lock is on the wed.

Table of Contents

Prelude 1

Keep Kissing 3

Little Things 18

Money 28

Two Words 43

Remember 50

She Lightning, He Thunder 57

Interlude 66

A Soft Answer 70

Communication 75

Expectations 86

Intimacy (see/into/me)	93
Raising Kids (parents only)	105
A Syrian Heart	112
Postlude	121
About the Author	124
Enhancement A	126
Enhancement B	129
Enhancement C	131
Enhancement D	139
Enhancement E	141
Enhancement F	142
Enhancement G	143
Enhancement H	147
Enhancement I	151
Enhancement J	157

Think of a number.
Double it.
Add twelve to the total.
Divide the total by two.
Subtract the number you started with.
The remaining number is _____.
(see Enhancement E)

(Regardless of the number you start with, if you will always follow this little formula the remaining number will always be this number.)

Prelude

This is a simple little book about love and marriage. It is simple because marriage doesn't need to be complicated. It is also little because it doesn't take a lot of reading to make a warm and happy marriage. And, in the economy of things, a little book should cost only a little finger and not an arm and a leg.

There are forces at work in the world seeking to hinder and destroy the love in marriage. The family is under siege because it is from a husband and wife that love and integrity and work and honor and respect and virtue and fidelity and faith and intimacy and accountability and manhood and womanhood are taught. The complexity of the world has siphoned out the simple foundational principles of marriage and too many couples find their love going nowhere in the cyberspace surrounding them. In a howling, high tech world floating on power and money, yet craving for simplicity, perhaps this little book will be a gentle wind. Madly in love marriages are here for the making. However, we have to want it, and we have to keep kissing.

Quite simply, marriage is more doing than anything else. Much like the equation two pages back, if we will do certain things, then the outcome will be correct. The only variable is that we have both a man and a woman working the equation. Oh my goodness!

(see Enhancement J)

Keep Kissing

Kissing isn't sanitary so the doctors say,
They looked into a microscope and found it out one day.
And though it's very interesting
when all is said and done,
A million germs and you and I
could sure have lots of fun.

source unknown

Let's face it, kissing rocks, or whatever other generational word moves you. I used to lay in bed at night

Keep Kissing

as a youngster thinking how fun it would be if I could ever find someone to kiss, or better still, find someone who wanted to kiss me. Mom was the only one that dared do it. Moms are so brave.

At age six, I wandered through the house one night searching for Mom. She always came in and knelt down beside me as I said my prayers. Then she would tuck me in and give me a big kiss, but not tonight. I couldn't find her anywhere.

"Mom," I yelled endlessly, "where are you?" Running down the hallway I entered my parent's bedroom thinking for sure I would find her there.

"Mom," I yelled again, but only silence. Dejectedly, I made my exit but heard a little mumble as I passed the closet. I grabbed the doorknob with excitement and pulled it open. There she was, hiding from me in the arms of my dad, and kissing, of all things. I felt immediately that I had entered the execution zone as I stood there frozen in the moment. As they broke their embrace I was out of there in world record time to my bedroom. I dove into bed with a giggle, feeling safe and loved because these 30-year-olds were kissing. I just knew they liked each other. People in love seem to kiss, and kissing seems to help people stay in love. That seems pretty simple to me.

By the time I was ten years of age many tall antennas began to appear on top of the homes. Television had finally come to our town and when we finally got our first television I saw more people kissing. I began going to movies and I noticed the music always got louder and more intense when the leading actors kissed. I began to think that if I want to be normal, I better learn how to do this.

"It looks pretty simple," I thought to myself, "and it just takes one of those other kinds of people, you know the kind that are nicer than boys. It looks to me like you just put your lips together and *voila,* a kiss is made."

Then I turned 14. I was in the eighth grade watching an assembly produced by my fellow students and Dixie started her dance. It was a modern dance and she wore these black mesh stockings with some kind of red accent. I don't remember what else she wore but my mind was in gear.

"Gosh, she is so cute, or something," I thought. "I think I would like to kiss her."

Well, I never did. But, I thought about it a lot, like every day. I asked my friend, Vic, a born Romeo who was dating by age 13, if he had ever kissed a girl.

"Yeah," he said. "Last night, me and Ruth Ann."

"What was it like?" I begged. "Tell me, tell me!"

"Wow!" is all he said, just wow. I began to wonder if I would ever have my own "wow" experience.

In my 15th year I took a major hit in my kiss quest. The class seating chart placed me directly behind one of the most beautiful girls in the school. All us boys had this rating system wherein we likened the girls to the great Helen of Troy who was so beautiful her face could launch a thousand ships, hence our rating scale became milli-Helens, a thousand being the most beautiful possible. This girl I was sitting behind was a 985, a real knockout, one of the top five cutest girls in the school. I was in heaven.

I would run to class every day, just to sit behind her and smell her perfume and stare at her back. She didn't know me from anybody and, of course, never said anything to me, but I was content just to be that close to her.

Then one day, as we were all doing some class work she turned around and I could sense she was staring at me. I didn't dare look up but I could feel her stare. I was faking everything I was writing trying not to notice but I just couldn't help it. I gradually worked my eyes up towards hers and finally our eyes met. There we were, staring into each others eyes, the first girl's eyes I had ever really looked into in my life. Right through the pupils of her eyes I looked into the depths of her soul. My heart was racing. This was wonderful. So this is what it is all about. I am in love, how incredible. I knew what she was going to say. My fantasies had already programmed me for it.

"I love you, Rand. Meet you out in the parking lot after school and we will kiss and kiss and kiss."

I waited. Thirty seconds I waited for her to tell me that. After eternity passed she broke the silence, having pulled me into her heart with her 985 rating. Casually, wrinkling up her nose as she looked into my eyes, she told me how much she loved me.

"Geeeeeee, you're ugly!" she said, shaking her head and turning back to her desk.

My eyes quickly went down to my paper where I continued faking what I was writing. I managed to maintain my composure on the outside, but inside I was drowning in my tears. I went home after school and locked myself in the bathroom and stared in the mirror, trying to find the ugly. Yup, it was all there, the long nose, the freckles, the ears, the eyebrows and crooked teeth. Even my hair was the wrong color. How was it that Mom and Dad had managed to keep this great secret from me all these years? But, there was no question about it. One of the top five girls in the school, a 985, had decreed it, and certainly it must be so. Kissless I would be forever.

For the next several months and even into years I would walk down the halls of school, ugly and all, singing *KISS ME, HUG ME, NEVER LET ME GO-O,* but no one ever wanted to. There were times when I even thought that someday maybe, if I was really lucky, I could find someone as ugly as me and that I wouldn't mind kissing her if she didn't mind kissing me. Then we could maybe even get married and go have a bunch of ugly kids, and basically have a good ole, ugly life forever.

Fortunately for me I had some other interests that didn't require one to be good looking. Football, basketball, baseball, debate, none of them cared a lick about looks. I even ran for a student-body office when a friend secretly submitted an application form with my name on it.

I turned eighteen my senior year in high school and had gradually learned to live with and love my freckles and other mutations. That's when I first saw her. I was conducting an orientation meeting for all new incoming students at our high school when she came through the door. My eyes riveted on her and no one else. She came down the right isle with such queenly grace and elegance I fully expected the royal court of trumpeters to sound her long awaited arrival. She made her way down to the middle of the room and then turned and walked towards the center. Never had I seen one so beautiful and breathtaking as was she. The thousand ships of Troy sunk deep in the ocean that day, for this young lady was far above that kind of juvenile jury. She was magnificence in motion, every single centimeter.

When school started the following Monday I passed her in the hall. I could see her coming my way in the crowd. I locked my vision upon her large chestnut brown eyes, taking a chance and remembering the devastation of the last girl's eyes I dared look into. We passed without a word, but our eyes acknowledged each other as she smiled at the nod of my head.

My winning touchdown and victory dance two weeks

later somehow made me a danceable commodity and I found myself surfing with her and the Beach Boys on the dance floor and our life began. From September to April we dated, not steady, but more with each other than any other. Oh, how I wanted to kiss her, but I didn't. I couldn't. I shouldn't. I wouldn't, until I knew she wanted to. I didn't want to chase her away and found myself singing, *"YOU'RE JUST TOO GOOD TO BE TRUE-UE, CAN'T TAKE MY EYES OFF OF YOU-OU."*

Sometime in April we had our first kiss. I know, I know, that's eight months from when we started dating. But I'm a slow mover, and when we did kiss it was ours. We have been kissing ever since. Now you tell me. Why does it have to end? Why do a husband and wife kissing have to shut down after two months of marriage, or six, or ten years or thirty? The fact is it shouldn't and it couldn't if we wouldn't let it. So, we men need to get off our duffs, out of the chair we are sitting on, out of the office we are working in, off the golf course we are hacking up, out of the ridiculous meeting we are suffering through, off the plane we are riding in and go kiss our wife. Right now, this very moment, get it done, do it, now. I'm not writing another word until we do it!

It doesn't matter if the plane has landed yet or not. Call her on that neat little phone in the back of that headrest in front of you and give her a kiss right over the phone and tell her you will continue it in exactly two hours and thirty-seven minutes when the plane lands, and it better not be late or you will sue every airline in America.

Yup, I just got up from my chair as I wrote the last paragraph and went to kiss my wife and she has gone to the store or something. I have this kiss waiting for her and if she doesn't get back soon I am going to sue every store in the city. Everybody else is, so why shouldn't I? A missed kiss is a kiss amiss, and that is dangerous.

Now have you got it? It's very simple. Just go do it. If you are a wife reading this, you go out there on the golf course and wait for him on the 14th green and then kiss him after he sinks his birdie putt and then watch his buddies fall apart the last four holes while your husband finishes birdie, birdie, birdie, eagle. Or, if your kiss is too powerful he might finish bogie, double bogie, triple bogie, and out of bounds on the last hole. Either way you win and so does he.

Now, just thinking about kissing every day is like swinging at a golf ball without a club. One can swing and swing but the ball never moves. I am inviting us to take some action and keep kissing every day. Husbands and wives that kiss a lot stay together a lot, a whole lot more than those that don't, besides having a ton more fun. It is a symbol that the two of us belong to each other and a reminder to both of us of the covenant that binds us together the day we were married, regardless of rain or sunshine.

I started this chapter telling about my parents and finding them kissing in the closet. It doesn't take very long to grow old and when I stopped in to check on them a bunch of years ago, I was no longer six and they were no longer in their thirties. Dad was well into his eighties now and had suffered a series of strokes leaving him very much alert, but bedridden. He spent his time in a hospital bed in his den, just off the kitchen where Mom could care for his every need. As I silently tip-toed into the kitchen I could see that Dad had raised his remote bed as high as it would go, and he had taken a passenger. Knowing him,

I am sure he lowered it to rock bottom and coaxed Mom into joining him for a ride. There they were, two lovebirds as always, kissing and hugging as they had done all of their life together, knowing all too well that their time to play such games was soon to be gone, at least for the moment. Now it was my turn to hide in the closet, as they did from me fifty years earlier. I stayed in the shadows just long enough to hear them talk and cry together and kiss and kiss and kiss. Then I left them together, as I did fifty years ago, with a giggle. After all these years they were still kissing, and so was I. Surely this is the way God intends it to be. Maybe, more than anything else we do in marriage, we should keep kissing. We loved it before we were married. Is there anything wrong with loving it after we're married?

****

Kissing so they say breeds germs,
They kill us by and by.
But tell me Darling, do you know,
A nicer way to die?

source unknown

Little Things

She looked at him, her heart a flutter,
As he carved **I love you** *in the butter.*

source unknown

On our wedding day the butter thought above was shared with us as we were encouraged to remember the constant reminders of love in our marriage, you know, the dumb little things we used to do while we were dating and courting. I love little, maybe because I have never been big. It is always a thrill to see a little player in the midst of the behemoths on the athletic field or court trying to avoid being squashed like an insect among the giants who are there mainly through inherited genes.

I have come to believe that in marriage relationships, a lot of little is more effective than a little of a lot. Or, in language more mundane, giving my wife a new Lexus once a year for her birthday is far less than giving her a tire one week, followed by the left rear door the next week, followed by the right inner-heated bucket seat the next week, and then the front left headlight, followed by the transmission, GPS system, and so on. Each week that I would give her part of the Lexus would be a reminder to both of us that I love her, and all of us need constant reminders or we forget. And besides, the anticipation of a completed car after watching it self-assemble before her eyes for a year would be like giving birth. Well, maybe not. But, fifty-two smaller reminders a year are much more powerful than one finished car on the doorstep. Or, if that example doesn't work for you, how about brushing your teeth for an hour at the end of the month, rather than two minutes a day for a month? Which is best? Or maybe drinking a big gallon of water at night is not nearly as good for us as drinking eight smaller glasses of water during the entire day. Obviously, almost always, a lot of a little is better than one biggie.

Just yesterday Shirlee brought me a little cup of chocolate cream pie, one of those samples given away in grocery stores trying to lure us into buying a whole pie overflowing with trans fats. I loved every carb, and even more the idea that she carried it around for two hours in her purse until she arrived home, and all for me. I was reminded that she still loves me.

Several years ago, because I was so tired of watching once happy marriages melt away with families and children being dissected by divorce, I went out and interviewed a ton of couples and had them fill out a little questionnaire on what it was that their spouse did, or what they wished they would do, to show them that they loved them. Most of the expressions of love were just little things, day to day actions of each to the other reminding them they are loved. I categorized all of these comments, added some fun words and came up with what I called **Spouse Spice.**

The blue spice bottle was for him and the red one for her, and inside were one hundred little cards, measures of love, suggesting what wives and husbands wished their spouses would do. Most of us know we're supposed to do these little things all the time. We just don't, or we forget, or we're too busy, or just too tired.

It was my hope that these ideas might spark a little creativity and fun in a marriage and prompt some actions between the two players. After all, the success of any game, any theatrical production, any venture into the future, will depend upon how well the players play it.

The success of any marriage depends completely upon how each of the players perform in their respective roles in relationship to the other. The following are a few examples from Spouse Spice:

His

- It is good to tell her that you love her, but talk is

very cheap. Love is doing. Love is action. Love requires motion. Love is movement. DO SOMETHING. Put some pomegranate juice in the refrigerator. Women love anti-oxidants.

• Seek her counsel on an important matter. She is your wisest counselor and sees things you cannot see. A woman's eyes are beautiful and wise.

• Her sexual needs are quite different from yours. Have you ever really discussed with her how you are meeting her sexual needs? Ask her. Be prepared to learn.

• Always help her on with her coat. Hold it low so she can put both arms in at the same time and then pull it up over her shoulders. Then bring your arms in around her and kiss her on the cheek. She will melt.

• Walk with her in the moonlight when the moon is full. Notice her beauty. Howl if you want.

Hers

• Support him and praise him in some project he is involved in. He can change the world if he knows you support him and have faith in him. Oh, how he needs your approval. It puts a big, broad, "S" on his chest.

• Whether his interests be sports, nature, opera, or travel, powerful binoculars make a great gift for a man. He may even look at you with them, bringing you right up close.

• Criticism annihilates self-esteem. It can snuff out the flames of love quicker than your local fire department, causing anger and rebellion. Build him, don't burn him.

• Blow him a kiss from across a crowded room. This silent, reassuring, provocative gesture lifts his spirit and strengthens his resolve and confidence that you are his forever.

- Dial Runaway Bay or someplace like it and capture him away for a fun weekend alone.

Think what a difference it would make if at least every few days each of us was doing some dumb, little, stupid thing to show our love. Dumb, stupid, and little reign supreme here.

Let's end this little chapter by going back to carving *I Love You* in the butter. The last time I did it a few years ago it made her day once again. Imagine if she was making seven peanut butter sandwiches every morning to feed your herd during school lunch time. However, at 6:32 a.m. on this morning, she opens the cupboard door and finds a cube of butter artistically carved with **I LOVE YOU** staring her in the face. It is easier to use the symbols, 'I', then a heart, then a 'U'. She will smile as she makes 100 sandwiches, well, maybe 30. It will warm her heart and she will use a fresh cube of butter and save the buttery love note. If you plan on becoming butter carvers, may I suggest that you freeze the butter before carving? It will hold its form much easier. Start out with the simple and powerful I LOVE YOU. When you get that mastered you can advance to a full pound cube of butter or even a five pound block of Kraft cheese. You could even try carving Michelangelo's statue of David or Moses or Mount Rushmore or the pyramids of Egypt to really make her day. The possibilities are endless.

Of course, I'm just kidding, kind of, but its incredibly fun trying to think of little things that say I LOVE YOU. It might be the only time in life when thinking little is better than thinking big.

Now, have we got this? Let's get it done, though it's never done, especially for us men.

(see Enhancement G)

****

Lots of little is a whole lot more than little of lots.

Money

He said, "You don't bake bread like my mother used to."
She answered, "And you don't make
dough like my Dad used to."

anonymous

Money makes monsters out of all of us. No matter how much we have we never seem to have enough.

Seldom do we go where we want to go, see what we want to see, do what we want to do, eat what we want to eat, or have what we want to have. The monster of it all is that everything takes money. Even doing nothing costs us money.

The only thing I brought to our marriage was some love and an old pale blue Karman Ghia with one head light, a mutation from the Volkswagen industry. The heater kept the windshield iced over through July, and periodically the battery would hold a charge through the night. We lived in a tiny, old, one-bedroom house on a canyon road paying forty dollars a month. We were poor college students living on love and a periodic overturn of the sofa hoping to find some loose change. Thank goodness we lived on the side of a hill where we could park our car pointing down.

"All right Sweetheart, make sure the key is on and I'll get us rolling."

"Now how fast do we need to be going before I pop the clutch?" Shirlee would ask.

"Not very fast, and I'll holler when you should pop the clutch. Just make sure it's in gear and the key is on when you pop it."

Off we would go, me pushing, and Shirlee behind the wheel with her foot on the clutch, ready to pop it. When I was out of breath I knew it was time to pop it.

"Pop it!" I yelled, "pop it, pop it!"

And she did, and the car started, usually, and that Karman Ghia was good for most of the day, until the next morning.

Those were good and wonderful days as we began to learn more about each other and about cars and how each of us run. Running behind that Ghia every day exhausted both our lungs and our legs and we felt one of our first great needs was a car that worked. I was employed part time as I finished my degree and Shirlee decided to postpone her education and work full time so we could join the twentieth century. We worked and saved until we had enough cash to buy a little light yellow Toyota Corolla Fastback. Oh, the influence of cash in hand. It empowers you to talk out of your feet, allowing you to walk out of anyone's office wealthier than when you went in. Otherwise the salesman controls your purse.

I had lots of figures and numbers written on my note pad. We had done some homework on cars prior to visiting the dealer, Shirlee being employed at a bank and knowing the true value of cars, loans, etc. Our fixed price for a new car was $2077.00 with tax, and not a penny more.

The first dealer listened intently as we told him what we wanted and the amount of cash we would pay for it.

"I can work with that," he said with a smile on his face.

As he submitted the papers for us to sign the total

price had risen to over $2800.00. I was shocked.

"All we have is $2077.00 cash and that is all we are paying. If you don't want it we will go find someone who does."

"Not a chance," he said.

We talked with our feet and walked out of his office and moseyed out to our car as he watched us all the way. I helped Shirlee in her side of the car, then opened my door.

Down the steps from the show room the salesman ran, "Wait a minute, hold on, hold on," he yelled as he arrived at my closing door."

"OK, OK," he said. "Will you drive it off the lot for $2087.00?"

I looked at my notepad, "I think it was $2077.00"

"OK, OK," he said as his eyes rolled back in his head, and that was OK with us.

There is just nothing like the power of cash. It is a screeching eagle, a lion's roar, a sonic boom, a hole in one. Forty-five years later and I just purchased a condo the same way. It is so fun to watch people's eyes when you tell them you are going to pay cash. It just kind of takes away their advantage and you become the bargaining chip. I know it is not always possible, but for almost everything except a house, paying cash will keep you debt free.

We are talking about filthy lucre here, the love of which is the root of all evil and canker of the soul. It is called money and I think we ought to make some, maybe a lot of it. Not a whole lot, mind you, but enough to offset the suffocating stresses that come with not having sufficient for our needs and wants. Money can't buy happiness as evidenced by all of the people we know who are rich and unhappy. But just thinking out loud, if one chooses to be unhappy, it is better to have some money to go along with the unhappiness than to not have money. And, if one chooses to be happy, why not have money and be happy rather than being poor and happy? If we have some money our capacity to do good increases and at least we can help those who don't have enough, making them happier. And what about those who are waiting for money before they get married? Here is their poem.

WEDDING DAY

The Bride, white of hair, stoops over her cane,
Her footsteps — uncertain — need guiding.
While down the church isle, with wan toothless smile,
The Groom, in wheelchair, comes gliding.
And who is this elderly couple, thus wed?
You'll find when you've closely explored it.
That here is that rare, most conservative pair,
Who've waited till they could afford it.

anonymous

Poverty either imprisons or empowers us so a little poverty during sometime in our life ought to get our brains working in the right direction.

IF YOU NEED SOME MONEY

I am not sure who Lord Wellington was but his eight simple words are the enemy of poverty. In some meeting while trying to decide something important he said, "We have no money, therefore we must think." The great God in heaven has blessed us with gigantic capacity to think and to solve problems and still the best ideas are itching to be thought of. If we are God's children, and we are, then it might not be a bad idea to ask Him for some help as we think.

He calls it inspiration and revelation, although you can call it what you want. But if I were you I would call it what He calls it. He expects us to think and make a difference. After we have thought about it, then we go to work. I have a thought above my desk penned by one of my heroes, Thomas S. Monson, which says, "You can think a thought to death, but until there is action, there is no change." He follows that great invitation with, "Work will win where wishy, washy, wishing won't."

The power to think and work has success and dollar signs written all over it. So maybe we ought to stop reading for awhile and go find a quiet closet and think. Just do it now. Stop reading for a few minutes and go think. Get out of here. Stop thinking about thinking and go think, really think, on your knees kind of thinking.

IF YOU HAVE MONEY THAT IS SLIPPERY

Money is so slippery it slides away faster than we

make it. It's slicker than a casino card shark with silicone fingers. The only weapon to down this demon is a BB gun. The first B is a BLOWTORCH. Gather all of your credit cards together, both major and store cards, and torch them. You have been told this before, but do it this time. As those colorful cards melt before your eyes, so will that suffocating monthly payment that steals your future earnings. Keep only one major credit card for emergencies, but never use it unless you put cash aside in an envelope to cover it immediately.

The second B screams for BUDGET. It is fascinating to me that everybody out there in the world seems to want my money. I worked hard for it and they are doing everything they can to take it away from me.

So, as I climb up onto my stagecoach which carries my fortune in a strong box and grab the reins, I want my budget riding shotgun to blow away the outlaws bent on taking my fortune away.

Budgets need no explanations. Just get one that works for you and follow it. Now it gets really tricky if both husband and wife are working and pulling money into the family strongbox. If one is making more than the other should they keep more for themselves? You'll have to make that decision. Two income families always present some difficulty, but here is some good counsel.

His monthly income	$4000.00
Her monthly income	<u>$3000.00</u>
Total	$7000.00
Monthly bills, expenses, savings	<u>-$5000.00</u>
Balance	$2000.00

The $2000 balance is equally divided between husband and wife, each receiving $1000 to spend as they desire.

Neither has to ask the other for money and each has the freedom to spend their $1000 as they desire. If my favorite sound is hearing metal pulverizing paper, then I am free to go over to the sink and drop my ten $100 bills of filthy lucre down the garbage disposal and not have to account for it to anyone. It is my choice. But once it is gone, it's gone. It has to last until the next pay day. There is something fun and wholesome and liberating about having your own money to work with without having to ask for it.

CHILDREN AND MONEY

Shirlee and I chose to have nine children so there wasn't a lot of money to go around. We had to think. Why not teach the kids how to work? What a novel idea. I can't even begin to tell how many newspapers, Shopper's

Guides, and telephone books we delivered over the years. All of my sons came through the same grocery store stocking shelves on the reputation of their older brother. There is nothing demeaning about children learning how to work and to work hard. It might be the greatest wealth a parent gives a child, almost equal to their mom and dad loving and kissing each other.

When we have money, the tendency is to shower it out upon our children by way of gifts because it gives us great joy to see them happy when we give it to them. It will take some outstanding parenting to keep kids in full bloom when they have everything they want. Be ever so careful on letting your children grow up having everything they want. I love the words of the great educator Neal A. Maxwell, when he said, "So many young people have had so much done for them they are totally done in." Think about it.

I saw a sign one day that read:
I STARTED OUT WITH NOTHING.
I HAVE MOST OF IT LEFT.

To me that sign was both a warning and an invitation. It is a warning that money is hard to hang on to and everyone is happy to take it from us if we let them. And, it is an invitation to protect and guard our future as we use money because money is only good if we use it. Don't try and leave a lot for our posterity. It will most likely hurt or destroy them.

If we have money or need money I share two recommendations.

1. Read George Clason's *The Richest Man in Babylon*, a quick read on obtaining wealth.

2. Watch at Christmas time every year the DVD *The Ultimate Gift,* a delightful family movie on the secrets of finding and using money.

*****

(See Enhancement F . . . For husbands only! Wives, do not go here. It will ruin everything. Just know that your husband is buff, maybe the buffest of all buffs.)

Two Words

The greatest gift ever, other than life itself, is the gift of words, for without them........................

If you were to choose two words more important than any other to insure the happiness and joy and success of a marriage, what would they be? Think deeply now. How about *fun* and *personality*, or *respect* and *trust*? Maybe *intimacy* and *intelligence* or *wealth* and *health*, or *sex* and *success*, *children* and *love*, *religion* and *faith*, or *thank you* are all very powerful. Obviously there are not just two words that are the most important to joy in marriage and all of the previous words mentioned bring their worth and wisdom to the couple. Let me add my two words to the table.

Having met with many married couples over the years striving to improve their relationships or to find again what they once had in their marriage, I have come to believe that two of the most important words to the success of a marriage are the words *repentance* and *forgiveness*. These are religious words, though they should not be confined to religion. They are absolutely critical in husband and wife relationships. The following is a typical dialogue with a couple in crisis.

"It's just not the same anymore. He used to be so caring and mindful of me. Now, I am just a fixture in the house. We never talk. We hardly ever go out any more. He just sits in front of that TV and watches movies and ball games. And, he always takes off on that silly motorcycle of his and never tells me he's going. I can't tell you how messy he is. He's worse than a teenager. It is obvious he doesn't love me any more."

"Well, you're never home long enough to talk to, or to say good-bye to before I go cruising, or to watch a TV show with. Ever since you took that silly job we hardly ever see each other. And I've always been messy. It didn't used to bother you, so why now?"

"It's always bothered me. I've just put up with it all these years."

And on it goes, the accusations, the points of contention, nipping back and forth at each other in some kind of dog fight. Sometimes the anger multiplies and I have to separate them like children. How tragic that two grown adults are unable to figure this out. In fact, a great middle-eastern scholar has said that the only reason we come to earth is to learn how to *repent* and *forgive*, or in common terms, to change and to allow others to change.

Every husband and wife that ever married needs to change some things about themselves that bothers the other and every husband and wife needs to forgive and forget the stupidity and failings of each other. If we would just learn how to do that there would be a whole lot more kissing going on.

Never have the following words been said from either the husband or wife when I have counseled with them. Never.

"Oh, Sweetheart, I am so sorry. I had no idea you were feeling this way and that I was doing this to you. Is there any way you might forgive me? If you can find it in your heart to do so, I can change. I know I can.

And I will work on those things that are bugging you. If you will be a little patient with me, I will probably make some mistakes again, but I know I can do better, and I will. I promise you I will. Please let me. I'm so sorry. I believe I am the one at fault here."

If one of them, just one, would say something like that they would make history and I would build a monument to their honor. They would walk out of my office in tears and in each other's arms and both seeking to change.

Repentance isn't a popular word nowadays. If we need to repent it means we have been wrong, and we never like admitting we are wrong. But, how can we get better unless we have been wrong? So, mistakes are OK if we improve. Come on, hubby and wifey, we can do this. It is so very simple, yet the pride of the world has made it so complex. Just think of something we are blowing to pieces in our marriage and that sends the love of our life into the south forty. Just stop doing it. Just stop it. Freeze it. Fry it. Bury it. Toss it in the deepest cavern of the ocean. Nuke it. It doesn't matter if we like doing it. That is irrelevant. We are stopping this thing because it is hurting the one we love and hurting the one we love is like hurting ourselves. Ouch! Really ouch!

Now let's not fool ourselves into thinking that our companion needs to reciprocate because they have a ton of things that they need to change. We can't control that. All we can control is what we do or don't do with our life. But the odds are very, very good that if we will repent and change direction then the other will forgive and then they will change some things. It is marvelously simple and that is the way it is supposed to be.

****

"A heavy storm of thunder, lightning, and rain. I had to remove the bed out of the wagon into the house. Lucy asked forgiveness for all past offenses. I forgave her and she forgave me and we determined to love more and more."

Thomas Bulloch Pioneer Journal

Remember

*When you look in the dictionary for the most
important word, do you know what it is?
It could be "remember."*

Spencer W. Kimball

Where were we when we first heard Elvis Presley, or the
music of the Beatles, the Bee Gees, or whoever was king in
our day? Can we remember exactly the circumstance and
how we felt at the time? Reach way down, far back into
the memory chips of our mind, you know, the ones with

the dust on them. Somewhere in there are some feelings, long forgotten, yearning to explode from their silent cells. There is power in the past, if we can remember.

When I was a high school sophomore my dad and I built a prize bedroom in our basement. I planned it myself. I had built in drawers, checkerboard floor, with my own study area, stamp collecting area, model building area, and short-wave radio area. Missiles and airplanes and rockets hung from the ceiling and all of my sports junk held up one wall.

At the head of my bed I glued a speaker on each of the bed posts, both pointing in toward my ears and I would lay there at night and listen to the radio.

"And now," the disc jockey said, "comes a new sound from Liverpool, England, The Beatles. I'm sure you're gonna like it."

"The Beatles?" I smiled to myself. "What kind of

name is that? They'll never make it with a stupid name like that."

Then those guitars and that drum started playing, and then the words came. I sat right up in bed.

"I love this. I love this song," I said as my hand fingered for the volume knob in the darkness.

"I wanna hold your hand, ya, hand. I wanna hold your hand. (drums)

And when I touch you I feel happy, inside.

It's such a feeling that my love, I can't hide, I can't hide, I can't hiiiiiiiiiiiiiiiide."

Every night I would wait for that song to be played. As I met and courted Shirlee the next few years that song became her. Whenever it played I thought of her. As she would walk into a classroom at school, the drums would beat in my heart.

And so it has been for the last forty-two years. Even

now, when that song rarely comes on the radio, I will swoon with the tune. I am generally driving in the car when I hear it and when it begins I will roll down the window, stick my elbow out, and be cool once again, cruising down the road, thinking of her and wanting to hold her hand just like I used to. Why should this be something *I used to do*? I loved that feeling then, and love it even more now.

When courting my bride, the bucket seats in my little car were always a problem. They kind of kept us separate and apart because that darn emergency brake stuck right up between the seats and it was like sitting on a sword. So, I always kept a little pillow in the car to cover the brake so Shirlee could slide over closer to me. But Shirlee would have to shift the gears because my arm was around her and couldn't reach the gear shift. I would push the clutch pedal in and she would pull the gear stick down to 2nd, and then up to 3rd, and finally down to 4th gear. As we drove along, we ground a lot of gears with her head on my shoulder, but that was just fine with me.

Now I ask you, why do I see so many young and older couples driving along with each of us pinned to our own door as far away from the other as possible? And what's more, we're not even talking. We are just staring out the front windshield in some sort of inner-vehicular, comatose trance waiting for our destination to somehow miraculously appear in front of us so we can get up the next morning and retrace our monotony. Of all of the Gods we may choose to worship, be they from heaven or from the world itself, I can't think of any who would advocate such benign functionality. The confusion of the world seems to smother all of us into silent, sitting androids instead of thinking, talking, people in love. When we were young and in love we were talking and laughing and listening to our music. Why can't we be old and in love?

All right, I've written a little about greasing up our memory banks. It means nothing unless we do something. So, this Friday night, why not remember some things about when we were so madly, head over heels, rock-sockem in love with each other. Why wait until Friday. I am now going to her. Really, I am. I am typing my last sentence and I am now gone to her to remember. (I just went into the bedroom and she is making her eyes look nice so I will wait a few minutes and then ask her to remember with me.) Maybe tonight, coming home from the movie, we will swing by the house where she lived forty-five years ago, and drive into the driveway and park the car. (I don't know who lives there now.) We will replay the first time we kissed. She will like that, and so will I.

****

If I could remember the word remember
I might remember to remember.

She Lightning, He Thunder

"My parents had not been out together in quite some time. One Saturday, as Mom was finishing the dinner dishes, my father stepped up behind her. "Would you like to go out, girl?" he asked. Not even turning around, my mother quickly replied, "Oh, yes, I'd love to!" They had a wonderful evening, and it wasn't until the end of it that Dad confessed. His question had actually been directed to the family dog, lying near Mom's feet on the kitchen floor.

Mary M. Trivigno, Reader's Digest, Dec. 1987
Used with permission.

No matter how we cut it, marriage is a gamble. Our dating days should have cut down the risk, stacking the cards in our favor because, hopefully, we have seen each other at our worst before we tied the knot. But, no matter how long we date we are never quite prepared for all of the differences separating the pink and blue. These differences have existed since Adam said hello to Eve so they must be inherent within us and serve some kind of purpose. Rather than roast our raisins trying to change these differences, perhaps it is best that we try to understand them.

Sometimes I talk with young couples getting ready for marriage. Their eyes are filled with stars and all they want to do is to not listen to me.

"I am so happy." she says. "I have found somebody just like me."

"Yeah, we're exactly the same." he says. "We both love

Chimichangas, UCLA football, and rollerblading down the streets of Palo Alto. We like exactly the same things and we are a perfect match."

While having some common interests and goals is certainly a good thing, why would I ever want to marry someone just like me? I would have to write another book and call it, <u>Agony of Agonies.</u> Why would I want another me in this world? Isn't one enough, maybe too much? I mean, if I had to sit across the room and look at me all hour, how cruel would that be?

I married Shirlee because she is so different from me. First of all she is built differently and is arranged much more pleasantly. She is a lot nicer to look at than my 190 pounds of misappropriated DNA. In fact, I think I contain three elements not even recorded on the Periodic Chart that hangs in front of chemistry class. I can sit across the room and look at her for days and never tire of it. She is so gorgeous.

We enjoy different music. When I get in a car that my wife has previously driven I always change the channel. I can only handle Mozart about once a year, twice at the most. When she gets in the car I have previously driven John Denver and his "Rocky Mountain High" quickly returns to the mountains. And when we both get in the car together it's a finger fight on the channel button. She is trying to find John Denver for me and I am dialing up Chopin or Mozart for her.

These differences ought to bring us closer together. Early in our marriage I bought her a wonderful birthday present. We still did our dishes in the kitchen sink in those days, and she commented on how nice it would be to listen to some music in the kitchen. Well, hey, I can handle that. For her birthday at the end of the week I presented her with a very nice portable transistor radio, one that I could listen to the ball games on also. I shall never forget her disappointment as she opened the box. I mean, a radio for her birthday? Am I that dense? Yes I am. What woman in her right mind would like a radio for her birthday? I would. That's because I was still in love with myself. I am learning that true love is really loving someone else.

A few years later I took courage again when I heard she wanted a purse for Mother's Day. I went purse shopping. Oh my goodness.

There are a lot of different kinds of purses, one for every day of the year, and also for morning and afternoon. It's incredible. I found this really neat brown leather purse with a huge pirate buckle on the side with two treasure chest hinges on the top. It is one of the sweetest purses I have ever seen. I loved it. It could hold all my tools and guns and still leave her plenty of room for her stuff. I shall never forget the look on her face as she opened her present to find the greatest purse I had ever seen.

I bought her some clothes once—she exchanged them. I bought some jewelry once, and some perfume—once. I've discovered this. It is easier for women to buy for men than for men to buy for women. And most men aren't very good gift buyers. Most women are great buyers; in fact, they are animals at it. This is good, otherwise I would spend my entire life in the same T-shirt and Levis.

Shopping is sheer boredom for me and such a waste of time. I can walk into a shoe store and buy a pair of brown shoes in less than five minutes. It doesn't matter if they fit or not. I just want to get it over with. I was looking at myself the other day in the mirror and noticed she had purchased everything I was wearing except my shoes. Perhaps this is the reason we see so many couples together where the woman looks like a million bucks and the man looks like loose change. I looked much better than OK because I was wearing what she bought me, and when she shops for herself, she always looks gorgeous.

Somehow gorgeous and opening your own door just doesn't go together for me. Now I know she can open a car door, but I can do that much better than she can and I enjoy it more. It is not a matter of being liberated and being able to do things for oneself. We all can do a lot of stuff on our own. It is a matter of a man being so happy that she is with him that he wants the world to know it, and he will show it by taking care of her every comfort without her lifting a finger. It is also a matter of her allowing him to treat her as a queen, and everyone knows that queens never open doors.

There is one little side note here for husbands. Watch how graceful a woman is as she gets into a car through a door you opened. They are sheer poetry in motion and so much not like us as we put one foot in, plop down with a thud, and then drag and twist our other leg until it is finally in. Notice how she sits first and then brings her legs into the car in one easy motion. And, as she does so, would there be anything wrong with commenting to her about how beautiful her legs are? I think not, as it will surely bring a smile to her face.

So husbands, let her do her thing. Let her be a woman. She is so good at it, and we ought to be thankful that she is. What I am trying to say is that I should cherish her feminine uniqueness and not try and change her to my likes and dislikes. I don't need another me in my life. I need her in my life and all of her marvelous non-Rand things. I trust she needs masculine me.

(see Enhancement A)

****

Physiologically a man's skull is thicker than a woman's skull. Maybe that is why men are so hard-headed.

Interlude

If we have a Prelude and a Postlude,
then we must have an Interlude.

My wife showed me in the paper this morning an article of a couple celebrating their eighty-second Valentine's Day. They recently visited the courthouse where they were first married hoping to get a photo taken. As one of the clerks pulled their marriage document they discovered they had been married illegally, to which the

96-year-old bride confessed she had lied about her age, she being only 15 when they were married.

"Yes," she admitted, "it is true I lied about my age that day. But, he sure was worth breaking the law for."

The 100-year-old husband begins each day by rubbing his sweetheart's back with the question, "What did I ever do to deserve you?"

His wife concludes, "He's still romantic, but most of all he's just a good man. Neither one of us has ever been bossy. I suppose that's what makes us click."

Deseret News, February 11, 2010

Why does a little story like this make headlines? Probably, because it doesn't happen very often, two people being madly in love after a century of togetherness.

Well, we are about half way through this little book and it hasn't taken long. I have tried to make it worthwhile and enjoyable reading without any guilt trips. You might conclude that I am an idealist, a non-realist, or a romantic and that I am living in a dream world. I'm not sure what I am, but I do know I like to be happy and I know what makes me happy. And, what is wrong with living your dream?

I am well aware that we all bring certain suitcases to the marriage whose contents are a composite of our upbringing, our experiences both terrific and traumatic, and our physical bodies. Some call it baggage, but whatever we call it, it's what we are. Sometimes trauma has affected our thinking, and experiences have tainted how we act. Sometimes hormones and chemical imbalances manipulate our mentality and we are ill physically or mentally and need some help to become well. These are times when trained counselors, doctors, psychologists, and experts in behavior can and should be most helpful to us in strengthening and positive ways. If you are ever in this mode I highly recommend you receive professional help from someone who is trusted and who reflects your own personal and moral standards. As in anything else, there are better or *worser* ones, as children say, and I would choose better over *worser* every time.

Well, lets get back to finishing this little book. We're *burnin' daylight,* as my cowboy father-in-law used to say, and if we're married and have some kids, we don't have time to let time dangle.

A Soft Answer

"A soft answer turneth away wrath…"

Proverbs 15:1

I raced out of the observatory as the thunderheads rumbled their way towards campus. Holding tightly to my books and papers I double-timed it towards the parking lot where I asked my sweetheart to leave the car. There was always an empty stall in one of the three long rows of cars in the lot so I knew it wouldn't be hard to find.

I arrived at the parking lot just as the rain began to fall but no matter. I would find the car momentarily and all would be well. Up the first row I ran as the rain began to pummel me. Down the second row I ran faster as now the storm had become a deluge. Up the third row I sprinted through the hurricane like wind and rain knowing that it had to finally be in that row. There were no other rows left. The car was not there.

Thinking that I had just missed spotting the car my first time around the lot, I back-tracked, only this time I was not running. Why run? I was already a walking sponge past saturation point. So I just walked and as I passed each car I became a little more displeased and drowning in self-pity. I finished my soggy replay the second time through and decided to just sit on the curb and get as wet and as upset as I could. I put my books and notes and papers on the ground so they could get ruined to the limit which undoubtedly would cause me to fail my class and then it would be her fault. As I sat there in my own wet depression, the thought occurred to me that perhaps she might have parked the car in the lot adjacent to the other side of the building. As I crept off through the storm to look at the other lot, sure enough, there it was in all of its glory. I dropped my books in her empty seat and watched the water ooze out on to the leather seat hoping it would ruin the place she sat most of the time.

All the way home I shivered and coughed, practicing pneumonia at every turn and rehearsing my cutting remarks to unleash upon the one I love more than anything else in the world. Why do we do things like this? What is it that causes us to want to hurt the one we love? I have no idea except that there are many forces at work to destroy anything that is good and beautiful.

I parked the car in front of the house and marched

toward the front door. Grasping the door knob I opened the door with authority ready to unleash my displeasure. At that moment I was engulfed with the glorious aroma of bacon and eggs and hashed browns as the love of my life leaned her head into the doorway and softly said, "Hi, Sweetheart, got your supper ready."

Now why did she have to go and do that? It ruined everything. Every sinister and calculated word vanished from my mind and heart and I was left standing in the doorway the dripping mess I had become. She took the sting right out of my heart with her gentle words and defused the verbal grenade I was about to throw.

Wasn't it Grandma that first taught us that if we can't say something nice about someone then don't say it at all? There is no need to pay a therapist $150 to tell us that. Any word that is meant to hurt or injure the one we love should never be spoken. When the writer of Proverbs penned the lines *a soft answer turneth away wrath,* he must have been thinking of husbands and wives.

Since that day in the rain my hurtful words have been locked away in some deep cavern of my mind. I've been saving them to use at some other appropriate time, but it has been forty-two years and I don't ever seem to have a reason. Perhaps I never will. You see, I love her, and one does not purposely hurt the one they love.

(see Enhancement I)

******

Love lasts longer for the less lippy!

Communication

*A man is driving up a steep mountain road. A woman
is driving down the same road. As they pass each other
the woman leans out the window and yells, "PIG!"
The man leans out of his window and replies, "WITCH!"
They continue on their way and as the man rounds the next
corner, he crashes into a pig in the middle of the road.
If only men would listen.*

St. Louis Fax Daily, November 8, 1999

We were living in Denton, Texas at the time, just north

of Dallas about 40 miles. Of my own free will and choice I was coerced and forced into becoming a Dallas Cowboys fan. It was either that or suffer a slow and untimely death, so I opted to cheer for the silver and blue. I was enjoying reading about them in the local newspaper one morning after I had mowed the backyard lawn. My youngest toddler tugged at my knee, so I am told, and asked:

"Daddy, is it OK to eat snakes?

"Huh?"

"Daddy, can we eat snakes?"

"Uh-huh."

I really enjoyed the sports page that morning, reading about the pride of Texas, and as I put the paper aside I vaguely remembered a little voice asking me a question. And then I remembered something about a snake. And then I remembered mowing the lawn that morning and running over a small snake in the grass and tossing it to the side to bake in the hot, Texas sun. My eyes doubled in size as I raced to the back yard in search of my youngster, only to see the tail of that snake disappear down his throat. He was smiling as I quickly looked around to make sure no one else was seeing what I just saw.

Let's face it men. Most of us are terrible communicators. Women of the earth, I apologize on behalf of all us boys for our blatant inability and disability of non-communicability. Please be patient while we learn this art.

I am a teacher by trade and talk all day to teachers, students, parents and anyone else who will listen to me. I get paid to talk. When I get home I am tired of talking. Many times as we stare at the ceiling before we slumber off for the night, Shirlee wants to talk. She hasn't talked with anyone all day, except maybe a two-year-old, a ten-year-old, and a fourteen-year-old. And since fourteen-year-olds don't talk, she has really only communicated with a couple of kids, not the most stimulating mind exercise. It is only natural she would want to speak with someone who really cares and is interested in her near death experiences of the day. We have had some very uplifting conversations as I gave her my total telepathy.

"Sweetheart, our youngest son about burned the house down today."

" How nice," I respond with my eyes closed.

"Twice."

"Perfect."

"And our little fourth grader has decided to get married this weekend. Is that OK with you?"

"No problem."

"She's nine years old."

"Sweet."

"I think I will fly to New York tomorrow and shop,

see a few plays and max out our credit cards. Are you OK with that?"

"Wonderful."

"And one more thing, sweetheart, I totaled the car today. I think I will get another one tomorrow. I am thinking Rolls Royce, maybe a Fararri."

"Uh-huh."

"Oh, and I forgot to tell you. I sold our home today, for 25 cents."

"Wowwwwwwwwwwwwwwwwwww. Way to go."

Why do our wives put up with us? Some of them don't, so it is imperative that we do better. It starts with us, men. We will find that if we will talk and communicate, then most often our wives will. Have we ever noticed that when we hold a little two-year-old on our laps and are talking, they will grab our face or cheeks and turn our head so they can see us as we speak. That one little gesture speaks volumes about communication. Whenever a wife, or a husband for that matter, is speaking to the other, drop everything—the newspaper, frying pan, TV, power drill, book, Blackberry—and look at them square in the face and focus on every word that comes from their beautiful lips. Pay attention. Focus in on every single word. Take our glasses off and look right into their face. It will likely blow their nylons right off and they will say, "Whoa, where did this man of mine come from?"

As newlyweds, while driving home from a movie I asked my bride if she would like to get some ice cream. She hesitantly said no, and so I drove home. It didn't take long to discover things weren't quite right.

"Is something wrong, sweetheart?" I queried.

"Oh, nothing important," she said. "I just wish we would have had an ice cream."

"I'm sorry. I thought I asked if you wanted one."

"You did, you did. But sometimes, when a woman says no, she really means yes. You haven't picked up on that yet?"

Quite frankly, I hadn't, and I'm still somewhat puzzled by that after a half century. But I really shouldn't be because we all kind of do that at times. Little wonder we are all a little confused as we say one thing and really mean the opposite. The fun of it all is we can learn to pick up the cues, the intonations, and pauses as we learn to really hear what the love of our life is saying.

Many times statements by one or the other are really questions or petitions for help. I was watching a ball game on TV one Saturday afternoon when Shirlee returned from grocery shopping.

"The car is filled with groceries," she announced as she entered our home through the garage door into the kitchen.

I can solve that problem, for men are problem solvers, and I am a man.

"Well, bring them in," I almost said because that is how one solves the problem. It only took me about 90 seconds to figure she was inviting, asking, begging me to help her unload the car. It would have been so much easier if she would have said, "Rand, can you please help me bring the groceries in from the car." I would have been all over it. But that is OK because after years of living with each other we are beginning to know exactly what the other is saying. And now, oh my goodness, we are beginning to know what the other is thinking without them even saying a word. It must be part of the process of becoming one. Undoubtedly, it could all be accomplished with greater dispatch if we men would listen better and we women would say what we really mean.

The only solution for not talking or communicating is

to talk and communicate and that requires us to open our mouths. Try saying something with our lips zipped and all we get is kind of a musical hum. So the solution is to open our mouths. Sometimes we can help the communication process by asking sincere questions that don't require a yes or no answer, which are dead-end questions. Better questions are:

What do you think about_____?
What are your feelings about_____?
Sweetheart, I need your help on _____?
What would you think if_____?

So, we must open our mouths, and most men should open theirs twice as much and maybe a few women should open theirs maybe half as much. The average man speaks about twelve thousand words a day, while the average woman speaks approximately twenty-five thousand words a day. I didn't know that.

******

TEEVEE

In the house
of Mr. and Mrs. Spouse
he and she
would watch TEEVEE.
And never a word
between them was spoken
until the day
the set was broken.
Then, "How do you do?"
said he to she,
"I don't believe we've met.
Spouse is my name.
What's yours?" he asked.

"Why mine's the same!"
said she to he,
"Do you suppose we could be....?"

source unknown

Expectations

*When a man marries a woman, they
become one; but the trouble starts
when they try to decide which one.*

Wisdom From Grandpa

"Are we ever really going to want to come out of our honeymoon cottage?" I thought to myself. "I mean really, why would anyone ever want to? Why not just stay in here and make love and kiss forever and stuff like that?"

Oh, the naiveté of youth, but I do remember thinking

that. There always comes a time, usually within 24 hours after crossing the threshold, when we unbolt and unbar the door and venture out into the dangerous and real world to discover that, yes, we do need to do other things beside sleep together. Do we remember those first few weeks and months of marriage when we expected our honeymoon to last forever only to have our expectations dashed? What were we thinking? We weren't.

Sweetheart, will you take the garbage out? Me? But I've always slept on the left side of the bed. Balance the checkbook? Are you kidding? I didn't know you had to change the oil in a car. Dad never allowed any of us to have our own charge card. Dishes, um, Mom always did them in our home, I think . . . don't we have one of those little machines that does them, or something? Why is the toilet always so gross? The car sure is dirty. I don't know how to iron anything. The shower sure is slimy. A dog, you actually want a dog? What's wrong with a night out with my friends every other week? So sports is #1 in your life? Can we get two televisions? I thought the vacuum was given to you as a wedding gift. Why do I need to get up with the baby? Who's doing the bills? Should I fix lunch or do you want to? I thought we were with your family last Christmas, and Thanksgiving, and New Years. I thought you liked sports. I'll plant the garden if you will weed it. It's only Monday, why are we having sex tonight? Don't you know I hate asparagus? I didn't know your Mom would call every night. Is it your turn to mow the lawn this week? I think there are 40 pounds of you I'm not married to. We danced a lot before we were married. So, you're a chocolamaniac. So, do you want to pray each night or what? You used to kiss me when you left. Do we have to camp out every month? Do we have to go to your church? Do I have to love the Dallas Cowboys? The living room is not the dirty clothes hamper. You didn't tell me you're a Democrat? I don't need you to open the door for me since I'm a big girl. I'm still going to open it for you since I'm a big man. Whoever has the remote in hand rules. Last one out of bed makes it. I'm the breadwinner, aren't I? What I earn is mine, maybe ours, maybe we split it. I didn't know you wanted me to initiate intimacy sometimes. If I could just figure out what makes you happy, I would be happy. Why don't we kiss like we used to, before we were married?

That was a long paragraph we just read. But it could be much longer. These are just a few of the expectations we deal with as lovebirds. In varying degrees the reality of marriage may be far different from what we expect it to be causing many to drop out early. Usually, we choose reality over expectations because it is easier. There is a better choice.

There are lots of people starving and dying around the world because of bad government and corruption. That is reality, but I much prefer the expectation, which is very hard. Most athletic teams never win the championship and never will without expectation. It is hard. Poverty exists because of reality and continues because expectations are never met. It is so hard to overcome poverty. Roughly half of all marriages shatter because people prefer to live in reality. Fun and happy marriages become reality when <u>realistic</u> expectations become the norm, and that is hard work. If our expectations aren't realistic then we talk together so they're not some fantasy out of Never-Never Land.

If a husband expects his wife to cook and clean, have babies, and be there for him while he brings home some money and plays ball and watches TV and enjoys 15 hobbies, then he needs to grow up. Sometimes wives need to grow up also because marriage is for grownups. Had Peter Pan married Wendy, he would have had to grow up. Wendy's last name could have been Pan, and there could have been some little Pans running around, had Peter's expectations been more realistic.

(see Enhancement H)

****

Many girls like to marry a military man — he can cook, sew, and make beds and is in good health, and he's already used to taking orders.

Wisdom From Grandpa

Intimacy
(see/into/me)

"It is more noble to give yourself completely to one individual than to labor diligently to the masses."

Dag Hammersjold, United Nations Secretary

Our wedding reception had finally ended. Standing in line, greeting people for nearly three hours, forcing a smile, trying to figure out where I knew that person from, and trying to act generally interested, is not my idea of a fun evening. Oh, we had a wonderful reception with delightful family, friends, and foreigners to enjoy it with; but it was more wonderful to have it over and to hit the road on our own, legally and lawfully wedded together.

I had wanted to be close to Shirlee almost from the moment I met her because there was something rolling through my veins wanting this thing called intimacy. It motivated me to pursue our friendship hoping to someday find out what love really is. I wanted it and thought a lot about it. I even read and studied about it in my university classes. I can't remember ever wanting or looking forward to anything more than to spend my nights with her.

We received a ton of presents that night and we would open them later. But tonight, we open a very special gift that comes not in a box. Some choose to open the gift early, before it is given to them, bringing disappointment, guilt, and other challenges and problems. Intimacy is God's wedding gift to the marriage and He gives it specifically for husbands and wives only.

After driving awhile we arrived at our honeymoon suite. What a thrill it was to gather her up in my King Kong arms and carry her across the threshold and through the door into our first night together. Since there were two suites beckoning us I reserved both of them claiming variety as the spice of life. The first suite sported an elevated bed with a wrap-around sheer curtain complete with motorized remote control. The second had a huge heart shaped hot tub large enough to swim in. I don't remember much about the décor, but I do remember her as we started to see into each other on our path towards intimacy.

There is a big difference between **taking** someone to be our lawful and wedded wife or husband, as most marriage ceremonies advocate, as opposed to **giving** ourself to the love of our life. So often the sexual relationship relies upon what we can take from someone, rather than what we can give to someone. We are gratified by the feelings we take from the experience and that has its own wonderful rewards. But not until we truly give our self completely to the other can intimacy occur. It has only taken me about forty years to discover that true intimacy involves more giving and less taking.

As we share ourselves and truly look inside each other we see what no one else has seen. We are special to each other and belong to each other and no one else. We kiss each other differently than we have kissed anyone else before. The word kiss derives from the Hebrew word *nasaq* which means *to kindle a flame*. Every man has learned that just thinking about a kiss ignites his fire but with her, many kisses in many places will help to set her forest ablaze. And it is good for every woman to know that his fire is raging through the forest while hers is just beginning, and to allow him some time to set her forest ablaze is a dream come true for him. And then again, there are times when his forest is only flickering and will require some extra time from her. There is a reason the forest burns differently at times for each of us, part of it generating an increase in our conversational intimacy. A man virtually reaches climactic satisfaction every time sexual relations occur.

Not so with women. Therefore, if a man will do all in his power to help his wife achieve sexual climax if she desires it, he will always receive his. The opposite is not necessarily true. Therefore husbands, we must become better lovers of our wives to insure that they are sexually receiving that which they desire and need.

Years ago, when I was teaching and counseling with

university students, many of whom were soon to be married, I attended a lecture by the renowned marriage and family therapist, Carlfred Broderick. During the question and answer time I introduced myself as one who counseled a lot with engaged couples and wondered if he could recommend a book that would help prepare them for marriage, and especially intimate relationships.

He smiled and said jokingly, "Well, I've written one, but I would never recommend it. Believe it or not, that's why we have honeymoons. One of the great problems of our prosperity these days is that we get married, usually between semesters or during a long holiday weekend, and think we have to travel to another continent or tour the entire western United States in less than five days so we can be back for mid-term exams by Friday. The finest teacher of intimacy is legal and lawful experience with communication."

Now here is a man who really knows his stuff. With all of his learning and endless interviews and counseling sessions, it was not about him and how many books he could sell, but about the bride and groom and what is best for them. He went on to say:

"What they really need is time together, in a room alone, with no deadlines to meet, where they can see and learn about each others bodies and talk with each other about themselves and what they like and what they like more in their physical relationships. This is light years better than any book they can read because when you read it in a book it is mainly just stimulating and nothing else. Intimacy can only truly be learned through being intimate without feeling guilty, and marriage provides that."

I have come to believe that one cannot teach intimacy. Experience is the teacher here. Dr. Broderick introduced me to a new word in intimate relationships of marriage. The word is *pleasuring*, and is defined as the giving part of marriage rather than the taking or the receiving. The husband and wife have the distinct privilege and honor of providing pleasure for each other, through touch and words and softness, in such a way that no one else can. The desire is not sexual climax, though that will always come, but the tender pleasuring time before that occurs wherein one or both helps the other enjoy the most magnificent feelings and divine sensation one's body can experience in this life. It is the time when femininity and masculinity join together in their finest hour, not only to bring forth life but to feel truly alive more than any other time.

The knowledge that this can and should happen on a regular basis binds a marriage together that is highly unbreakable. In fact, as one therapist mentions, *it is the very glue that holds a marriage together.*

Now, all of us are getting older, and we seem to have to coax our bodies to function as they used to. Intercourse can become a rare and even painful experience as early as forty and surely into our fifties and sixties. If the glue that holds a marriage together is gone, and intimacy has vanished, many couples fail to stick together. Infidelity and divorce tramples upon the lives of many through their forties and fifties as couples think they must find intimacy elsewhere. Other things can hold a marriage together, and they should; but next to eating, the desire to have intimacy in our lives is one of our greatest needs. And why would we ever want to lose the only gift we have left from our wedding day?

We live in a day of great knowledge and truth. Our individual bodies and our marriages can benefit greatly if we will take advantage of what we have come to know about aging. With a little hormonal assistance, a woman's intimate experience can be easy, comfortable, and more satisfying than ever before as her title changes from Mom to Grandma. Husbands, after their body has headed south, may have similar needs, and with a little adjustment intimacy can be as fun as their first nights together, and probably a lot more fulfilling. Any hormonal replacement does bring risks, so competent medical advice is imperative. We all need to take responsibility for our own sexuality because it so intimately affects husband and wife happiness.

Now, lest you think of me as one overbalanced on the physical, I am well aware that any husband and wife using sex as its foundation and reason for marriage will crumble like a momentary house of cards. The physical relationship is just one of the many pillars upon which a marriage is built, but it is one of the king beams. There is so much more to a happy marriage than sex, but probably nothing with the potential of being so binding and enjoyable.

And so, we returned from our honeymoon and opened a living room full of presents. Why does everyone think we need a toaster? It only took a few years and every gift we received that night has vanished or was broken or has been given to someone else for their wedding present. Everything that is, except the gift that God gave us, the gift of intimacy. It is the only gift that remains from the day we were married, and somehow I find myself hoping that it will be with us forever.

Well, I'm not quite sure how we did in this chapter, or if it is what you wanted or needed. Intimacy is not easy to write about since so many have varying opinions of it. But surely you can farm the kids out for a night or two and find a place called Runaway Bay and talk and intimate with each other. Regardless of your opinions, I think all will vote for that.

Oh, and one more thing. It is surprising how many husbands and wives like to hide themselves in the dark during their intimate time together. Though some couples prefer this, others may not. Which does your spouse prefer?

(see Enhancement D)

****

"Woman, without her, man is a beast." and,
"Woman, without her man, is a beast."

Raising Kids
(parents only)

*As arrows are in the hand of a mighty
man; so are children of the youth.*

Psalms 127:4

After raising nine of them, I ask myself the question,
"If I could share just one thing with parents that might
be more important than any other, what would it be?"
Since children are the most noble outcome of marriage

and since children have a way of making our marriage very happy or extremely sad, I offer a few words on their behalf.

The school guard, Big John, unlocked the door, and I entered another world. This was a lockdown school, and none of these boys wanted to be here. They were miserable and hateful free spirits who had given their parents and society more than they could handle. That's why they were here, a school for troubled boys, and this was my first day as their teacher.

Big John locked the door behind me and escorted me down the hallway to my first period class.

"I'll be out here in the hallway at my desk if you have any trouble," he said, smilingly.

I had faced tough kids before, but never so many of them all together. I was not afraid, though very much interested to see what kind of warfare would work on this battlefront. I was in enemy territory and I was stoked.

The little hellions lived up to their billing as I maneuvered my way through the first day. I noticed one thing that was the same in each class. There was a phone on the wall next to the marker board in the front of the class, and every time I would get close to it the class would quiet down to almost total silence. When I was on the other side of the classroom, away from the phone, the noise increased and bedlam would begin.

"Why don't you just pick up the phone?" said one of the boys after my last class.

"Why?" I responded with questioning eyes.

"As soon as you pick it up, Big John comes in and yanks them out of class. Just pick it up and he'll be right there."

"Thanks for the heads up, Tony," I said as our hands hit high. "You're the man."

I walked out into the hallway and noticed several of the boys standing at attention, straight and solemn, looking at the wall in silence. As I passed Big John's desk I stopped.

"What are they doing?" I asked inquisitively.

"What does it look like?" Big John fired back. "They're staring at the wall. These are the ones who were trouble in class today. Most of them are new and haven't learned yet. All the boys who come here have never had to be accountable for their actions their whole life. We can't teach them anything until they learn accountability. So, we put them in front of a wall for five hours or so."

"Does it really work?" I queried.

"Have you ever tried to manipulate a brick wall? If they want to stand in front of a brick wall for an entire year, that's fine. I can make it happen. It's their choice. If they are trouble in class, they stand in front of a brick wall for five hours, or all night long if they keep causing problems. But when they look out the window and see their buddies playing ball outside, skate-boarding, throwing Frisbees around and watching TV, they figure it out. To do that, they have to be good in school. It usually only takes a few days and then, for the first time in their lives, they become accountable for their actions. We can't teach them anything until they learn this law, and life will be really cruel to them until they do."

As I drove home that night, and many nights since, I have contemplated the message taught to me by Big John and all those rambunctious boys, particularly as they walked across the stage at the end of the year to receive their graduation diploma and enter society as builders rather than wreckers. The method used seemed very familiar to me, but I knew not why until I was one day reading about the creation in the book of Genesis and God working with His children, our first parents. God gave them a commandment not to partake of the tree, gave them the consequence if they did, and then allowed them their agency to make a choice with also the consequences that came with their choice.

So, when Adam and Eve chose to partake of the fruit they also chose the consequence and were cast out of the Garden and would later die. The power of the consequence of their actions taught them to be accountable. Otherwise they would have learned that they could get away with anything without suffering consequences of their choices.

Above all other things we teach our children, I can think of nothing more valuable, regardless of race, creed, color, or religion than to learn this one law; *I am accountable for my actions and when I make a choice, I also choose the consequences.*

****

Your sons will marry someone else's daughters, and your daughters will marry someone else's sons, and all that's left is you and the one you're married to, forever.

(As a teacher of teachers I have read countless theories and articles on discipline. There is some good in all of them, but none are as good as the simple process used by God with His children. If it was good enough for our Heavenly Father to use with our first parents, it ought to be good enough for us. To further see this law at work, turn to Enhancement C.)

A Syrian Heart

"Young men's love then lies
Not truly in their hearts, but in their eyes."

Shakespeare

Three Iraqi spies hung motionless in The Square as Shirlee and I entered Damascus, Syria in early summer of 1977. The four hour bus ride from Jerusalem had been hotly interesting as we journeyed to a street called Straight identified by Paul the Apostle in the New Testament. Three different times during our journey our bus had been stopped and emptied by machine-gun carrying soldiers of the Syrian army, our passports and backpacks checked, and our Arab guide pleading our cause as teachers from America who meant no harm.

After eating at the famous Ali Baba's middle-eastern restaurant, we came to the street called Straight and entered a large marketplace. A huge man-powered loom was creating beautiful tablecloths of every imaginable color causing Shirlee to linger longer. I left her amongst the tablecloths to bargain with the merchants and I retreated to the far end of the marketplace to bargain for some little curved blade Syrian daggers for our sons to poke themselves with.

After the deal was sealed I wandered back to the loom with its many colors, only to find that my bride had vanished. I searched everywhere fearing she might have been kidnapped. I stepped up onto a little pedestal so I

Keep Kissing

could look out over the entire marketplace, and there she was, on the complete opposite end from where I had left her. She was talking with a couple of Arab men, one of them being a sheik of some kind, dressed in a beautiful white khafia, Omar Sheriff mustache, a handsome handful of royalty.

As I pondered their conversation for a moment a totally off-the-wall thought bounced into my mind. It wasn't original with me, but planted there by a colleague of mine if ever I found myself in Damascus, Syria. I smiled as I stuck those three little mini-daggers in my belt and made my way over to where they were talking. Shirlee seemed relieved that I had come as I held out my hand to shake his hand. Shirlee introduced me as her husband as our conversation began.

"Oh, here he is now," she said. "I would like you to meet my husband, Rand."

"Ahhh, your husband. Hello. You have a very beautiful wife."

"Well, thank you very much," I agreed. "Would you like to buy her?"

His face danced with awe at my statement and with eyes as big as Frisbees he said,

"You sell her, you sell her?"

Now let me stop right here and say something before you judge me too harshly. I would never sell her. There isn't enough in the universe to even prompt a thought of it. I am just having a little fun here, something I will be able to tell our kids and grandkids about some day. And, how fun would it be to know what she would be worth on the open market?

He repeated to me, "You sell her, you sell her?"

"It all depends on how much you will give me for her," I said.

The sheik went dead silent as my fantasies took charge of my mind. Thirty seconds, maybe forty-five passed as he stared at the floor as I anticipated his robust offer. I expected the offer to be earth-shattering, maybe half of Syria, or quite possibly a thousand chests of rubies and gold, or maybe even ninety-five hundred camels?

"Rand, come on," she fearfully said as she wrapped her arm around mine and began jabbing me lightly in the ribs.

"Shirlee," I responded with a smile. "Let us do our business."

He raised his head to speak, and as he looked into my eyes I knew my anticipations were about to be realized. Whatever it was, it was going to be huge. It would be massive, the mother of all offers, and I would then tell him that it was not enough and we would walk away with a fun story. Little was I ready for the bomb he was about to drop. He spoke firmly, yet softly.

"I . . . give you . . . my . . . heart . . .for her," came the words in his broken English. What a letdown. It was a body slam to the desert floor, a punch in the paunch, a scorpion in my shoe. At the very least he could offer a ball point pen, some bubble gum, or a half empty barrel of oil, but his heart? What kind of offer is that?

"What would I do with your heart?" I jokingly responded as he watched me carefully and sensing my disappointment.

"You do not understand," he said with sage-like wisdom. "In our country the heart is everything. It is the finest I can offer, the supreme gift," pointing heavenward to Allah. "Again, I say, I give you my heart for her."

"She's not for sale," I quickly replied, since I was the only one smiling. "I'm just having a little fun here, a jolly time, a little joke."

"I thought as much," he responded. "You not want to sell her."

"No," I responded, somewhat embarrassed, "I most certainly would not."

My newfound sheik friend then began to smile and we had an enjoyable few minutes as we learned more about his customs and ancient land. As our group readied to leave we exchanged pleasantries and bid him farewell. As we started to walk away he pointed his finger at me and taught me again. He spoke to Shirlee.

"If he ever unkind to you, come to me. I make you a queen."

I shall never forget that look of contentment that swept across the face of my precious love as she heard those words and visually flung a soft dagger silently my direction. I know, I know, I deserve worse, but I learned what everyone needs to learn about love. Washing through my mind forever now are the words of a Syrian Sheik: "*In our country the heart is everything, it is the supreme gift...*"

When we love with all of our heart as we have vowed to do, we love with everything we have. No half pie love is acceptable. We love them with all we have, every molecule of our being, the whole pie kind of love. It is the *drop us in the desert* kind of love where scorpions and thirst and destruction are the only options before us, yet we try till we die to return to the love of our life because being with them again is all that matters. It is a love that is invincible and eternal and irrefutable, worlds without end. With God it binds us to each other forever with a bond that cannot be broken, and that is what it means to love each other with all of our hearts. Such is what I learned from a nameless sheik on a desert day in Damascus, Syria.

(see Enhancement B)

****

*To love, so as not to be loved in return, exalts
one to the highest realms of the universe.*

Postlude

Once upon a time there was a very ordinary and less handsome man who fell in love with a most beautiful woman, far exceeding his most secret and wildest dreams. After they were married they kept kissing and doing little things for each other while making a decent amount of money. With practice they communicated better over the years, and when they were wrong they repented and when offended they forgave. Remembering how they felt when they first fell in love, they admired their differences while answering softly when the other was angry. By solving their problems, reasonable expectations became their reality, intimacy their constant communion, and children their heavenly heritage. And through the din and dang of life they loved with all their hearts and kept right on kissing.

Wow, I just said in one paragraph everything I wrote about in the book. Maybe I should just print up a bunch of cards with this paragraph on it and sell them for a quarter. Love and marriage need not be complicated or expensive. It is basically *doing* and working hard at it.

So, come and dance with us, whatever dance you're doing these days. Dancing is a man and woman, two bodies moving with the music, together as one, and the feeling is sublime.

About the Author

Rand H. Packer and his wife, Shirlee, have been happily married for over 43 years and are the parents of 9 children. Rand has been a teacher in the public and private sector for 39 years and has lectured extensively throughout the United States and Canada.

He is the founder and CEO of Spouse Spice LLC, a business dedicated to strengthening and helping the love relationships between husbands and wives and believes the sweetest sweet in all the world is a marriage more madly in love from year to year. Husbands and wives are invited to visit **www.spousespice.net** for special gifts and ideas pertaining to love and marriage.

If we have not love, then what have we?

Keep Kissing

Enhancement A

I have taken some heat over the years, and more recently as I continue to teach marriage and family classes, that it is a marvelous gesture of respect for a man to open the door for a woman. Every now and then a woman gets quite disgusted with me as I do so but most seem very surprised and appreciative. Perhaps this little message from Dr. Samuel DeWitt Proctor will justify my continuance of such a holy act.

What Message is Sent By Good Manners?
One of my white students entered an elevator that I

was in already, and I removed my hat. "Dr. Proctor," she said, 'why...did you take your hat off when I got in the elevator? You're living in the Victorian age." She laughed congenially.

"If you'll get off the elevator with me for a moment, I'll tell you." At my stop, we both stepped off.

"I'm not a Victorian, I said, but some things stay in place from one generation to another, and certain manners stand for values that I hold dear. I believe that a society that ceases to respect women is on its way out. Women bear and raise our children, they are bound to them in early infancy, they need our support and security through this process. When we forfeit that, the keystone of family and home is lost. When we neglect and abuse women, the family falls apart and children are less well parented, and they fill up the jails and are buried in early graves. I believe that respect for women is the linchpin of the family and the society. Therefore, when you entered the elevator, I wanted you to have automatic, immediate, unqualified assurance that if the elevator caught fire, I would help you out through the top first. If a strange man boarded and began to slap you around and tear your clothes off, he would have to kill me first. If the elevator broke down and stopped between floors, I would not leave you in there. If you fainted and slumped to the floor, I would stop everything and get you to a hospital. Now, it would take a lot of time to say all of that, so when I removed my hat, I meant all of the above."

Tears sprang to her eyes. There are some values that abide. They have no racial or ethnic label.

Samuel DeWitt Proctor, The Substance of Things Hoped For: A Memoir of African-American Faith Manners Matter, L.R. Church (used with permission)

Enhancement B

On the inside of my son-in-law's wedding ring my daughter inscribed the words *ezer knegdo,* which interpreted means "*to find oneself.*" In the beginning God created Adam and his help meet, Eve. The word, <u>help meet</u> means, "*to find oneself.*" Perhaps one of the sweetest gifts we find when we are married is the package containing each other. You see, before I was married I thought I knew what love was. Love was me and all that I wanted. I was my own definition of love. Personal definitions are very, very risky.

After I married her, and all these many years, I have

been finding myself and who I really am. How many times each day do I think of her? I don't know. Do numbers go that high? From our very first dance my flag has been captured. Her very image is branded forever upon my soul, filling me with a sense of arrival. Her image rests constantly on the horizon of my mind. I see her there, encouraging me, beckoning me, motioning me to come. She picks me up with her gentle smile when I stumble. Her laugh enlightens me. I feel her hand on my face as the journey becomes hostile and as I trudge laboriously and forever onward. Cloudy days are counter to her countenance, and the knowledge that her embrace awaits my return muffles every sound of thunder. She is mine, so very much all mine.

Ah yes, and I have finally discovered a big portion of myself. I have discovered who I am. I am . . . hers.

Enhancement C

Case Study 1

"Dad, I want to buy a beagle and raise her and then have puppies and sell them and make money."

"Son, that's a great idea and I think you ought to do it. Maybe this weekend we will head into the city and find a nice pure-bred female Beagle and we will both become millionaires."

We found a nice little puppy with a good pedigree and papers and purchased her for $100. The first few weeks were fun, and little Fiesty followed my son wherever he went. As we hit the second month, she wasn't as cute and small anymore and a regular pain cleaning up after. My sweetheart became the heir-apparent for watching after Fiesty and that wasn't in the contract. So, I pulled my son into the living room and we talked.

"Son, how's Fiesty doing?" I asked.

"Good Dad, really good."

"I thought you were the one that was going to take care of her," I pressed further.

"What do you mean, Dad?"

"I understand that Mom is doing most of the feeding and clean-up."

"Well, I know she's doing some of it."

"But she's not Mom's dog, she's your dog. Mom's got plenty to do taking care of all of us. Don't you think because she's your dog that you're the one that should feed and take care of her? She depends on you for her life. That is your responsibility. If you need us to help you when you're away, just let us know and we will, but Fiesty is totally your responsibility."

My son wasn't saying much, but he was listening while looking at the floor. He had discovered that puppies grow up and become dogs, and they are not nearly as cute and fun.

"Tell you what, son. I think it only right that if you don't feed and keep her watered and cleaned up, then you have decided you don't want to have Fiesty anymore. It is up to you; it's your decision. Understand?"

I repeated our little agreement to him as he left the room so he completely understood and thought we had solved the problem. Wrong. A week or so later I came home and Shirlee said that he had gone fishing for a few days with Grandpa.

"Did he make arrangements for Fiesty?" I asked,

134   *Keep Kissing*

hoping for the best.

"I don't think so."

I was crushed. I thought for sure he would get it done. But he didn't, so now comes the hard part. Administering the consequences is always the tear-jerker, but if we don't, our children learn to do whatever they dang well please and then society breaks down. I started making plans to act upon his choice, for he had chosen to not have Fiesty anymore. After supper the phone rang, and there was a little boy crying on the other end.

"Dad, I forgot to make arrangements for Fiesty!" (more crying)

"I know son," I said disappointedly, loving every second of it because I knew what was happening. He had just become accountable for his choice and actions.

"Dad, do you think you could take care of her till I get home Saturday? Could you do that?"

"Son," now I was crying. "I would be happy to. Thanks for calling. Give Gramps a hug and catch a lot of fish. I'll see you Saturday."

I jumped in the air with clenched fist and hollered at the neighbors. A son had grown up that night as Gramps had to search the mountains to find a working telephone. I slept well. For the next several years, never once did we have to remind him to take care of Fiesty. When the responsibility is kept on their shoulders and they know they are accountable, they almost always perform as we hope.

Case Study 2

I had a big athlete killing my class on a daily basis because he thought he was God's gift to the world. I tried everything before I pulled him into my office.

"Simon, you're destroying my class. You can destroy others on the football field, but not in my class. If this happens again, you've decided to involve the football coach in this discussion."

"You gonna call Coach?" he grumbled.

"I'm not going to do anything, but you are, and I'm telling you, if you kill my class anymore, you have chosen to involve Coach in our next discussion. You're calling the signals here. Got it?"

We never did have a discussion with the Coach because Simon became accountable.

Case Study 3

I am grateful that none of my children had enough money to buy their own car while still in high school. I much prefer them to use my car because it binds me to them a little more. During the teenage years I am fighting for all of the good relationships I can get before they are about to blast out of our lives. So, what do we do when our teenager drives our car into the garage just before the sun comes up?

"Hey son, how's my car working for you?"

"Great, Dad. I really appreciate it. All my friends wish they had one like it."

"I'm delighted to have you use it, son, and you are welcome to it whenever I don't need it. You need to understand something about my car. It turns into a pumpkin at 1:00 a.m. every morning. It needs to be in the garage by that time, and you really ought to be home by that time anyway. I'll keep it filled with gas, pay the insurance, and have it glistening in the moonlight, but it needs to be in by the first hour of the morning. If it is later than that, then you've decided not to use my car. It is totally up to you. It is your choice."

"But what if we're running late, or cleaning up after a dance, or out eating or something."

"No problem. Just give me a call and we'll make the adjustment. Can you work with that?"

There is nothing I like better as a Dad than to receive a call from one of my kids telling me they will be home a half hour late. Remember, keep the responsibility on their shoulders, establish the rules with them, give them their agency, and make sure they know the consequences. Keep it fun.

Enhancement D

Many couples communicate very well and can talk comfortably and freely about their sexual relationships. Most, however, are somewhat hesitant to initiate sexual discussion and sharing of their intimate feelings. This little questionnaire may be of help. Both husband and wife should fill it out and discuss it together in bed as they share their answers and feelings.

1. With 10 being the highest, how much do you think your spouse enjoys sexual relations? _____

2. How often do you think your spouse likes to have intercourse?_____

3. Concerning sexual relations, which does your spouse prefer?

Planned_____ Spontaneous_____

4. What part of the sexual relationship does your spouse enjoy the most?_____

_____

5. What is it you wish your spouse would do more of to help satisfy your sexual needs? _____

_____

Enhancement E

6

Enhancement F

———❧———

Wives stay out of here.
For husbands only — the message is in line five.

Abcdefghijklbillscq!rwtuvwxyzabcdefghijklm+n
opqrstuvwxyzabcdefghijklmnppqrstuvwxysabfk
yuwdjqweirotpyulkjxvzbnamvljkhoyufodrlkhha
grtaqw%oeirutfdjkasl fjdkladfkj djfklasjpadjkeid
bcputlskakfiftylvbx$klocbillqmyinbdherdyiushoe
calskdjfhgzmxncbvqpwoeirutyalskdjfhgzmxncbvp
qowweurytlaksjdhjfgzmx@ncbvqjwmkriufvvzbm
klleopkpfnirjghbvncmmzqwertyuiopml

Enhancement G

HOW LOVE CAME BACK

Tom Anderson, Guideposts, August 1985

I made a vow to myself on the drive down to the vacation beach cottage. For two weeks I would try to be a loving husband and father. Totally loving. No ifs, ands, or buts.

The idea had come to me as I listened to a commentator on my car's tape recorder. He was quoting a Biblical passage about husbands being thoughtful of their wives.

Then he went on to say, "Love is an act of will. A person can choose to love." To myself, I had to admit that I had been a selfish husband – that our love had been dulled by my own insensitivity. In petty ways, really: chiding Evelyn for her tardiness; insisting on the TV channel I wanted to watch; throwing out day-old newspapers that I knew Evelyn still wanted to read. Well, for two weeks all that would change.

And it did. Right from the moment I kissed Evelyn at the door and said, "That new yellow sweater looks great on you."

"Oh, Tom, you noticed," she said, surprised and pleased. Maybe a little perplexed.

After a long drive, I wanted to sit and read. Evelyn suggested a walk on the beach. I started to refuse, but then I thought, Evelyn's been alone here with the kids all week and now she wants to be alone with me. We walked on the beach while the children flew their kites.

So it went. Two weeks of not calling the Wall Street investment firm where I am a director; a visit to the shell museum, though I usually hate museums (and I enjoyed it); holding my tongue while Evelyn's getting ready made us late for a dinner date. Relaxed and happy, that's how the whole vacation passed. I made a new vow to keep on remembering to choose love.

There was one thing that went wrong with my experiment, however. Evelyn and I still laugh about it today. On the last night at our cottage, preparing for bed, Evelyn stared at me with the saddest expression.

"What's the matter?" I asked her.

"Tom," she said, in a voice filled with distress, "do you know something I don't?"

"What do you mean?"

"Well, that checkup I had several weeks ago . . . our

doctor . . . did he tell you something about me? Tom, you've been so good to me . . . am I dying?"

It took a moment for it all to sink in. Then I burst out laughing.

"No honey," I said, wrapping her in my arms, "you're not dying; I'm just starting to live!"

Enhancement H

I was twelve years old when the dual track, army surplus jeep rolled over into the river, killing my grandfather. I came close to dying with him. I vividly remember my grandmother's grief as she was informed of the accident and the loss of the love of her life. She cried for days realizing their life together had suddenly come to a lonely tunnel that she would walk through her remaining years.

Life had not been easy for Grandpa and Grandma. They worked hard every day, eking out a living any way they could through the Great Depression and most other years. Seven children had blessed their life, five of them only for a few minutes. Life was very challenging and difficult, but they were committed to each other through the heck and hard of it all. They solved their problems and waited for the next ones coming around the corner.

As I read about their parents and their parents before them, they all seemed to have similar scenarios with two common factors. Life was hard, and they loved each other through it. The covenant that bound them together in marriage bound them together through the thick and thin of it all with an irrefutable commitment to each other. Marriage was not for the weak or the timid, nor the selfish and sedate, but those with real love flowing through their varicose veins.

I am well aware that today is a different century than that of our grandparents, but modern society hungers for commitment as practiced in days of yore. Many enter marriage today with the *I WANT IT NOW* attitude, that took our ancestors years of work to attain, both temporally and learning how to love. *Bailout* has become the catchword of the day and rather than solving little problems we opt to create bigger ones. Divorce sometimes may be justified, but when people are committed, a little tweaking can usually lead a husband and wife to the literal pot of gold at the end of the illusive marriage rainbow. It just takes some work, maybe some hard work, but that never hurt anybody because anything worthwhile takes work.

Maybe one of the greatest movie lines ever comes from a very mediocre film of several years ago. Tom Hanks, the rachety coach of a girl's baseball team in *A League of Their Own* rolls his eyes as one of the girls starts crying, complaining that it is so hard. Then, the line of the ages: "It's supposed to be hard," says the coach. "If it wasn't hard everyone would do it. **It's the hard that makes it great!"**

Life is hard. Sometimes marriage is hard, and family is hard, and profession is hard, and just getting up some mornings is hard, but not always. One of the reasons marriage is so great is that life is so hard. No matter how hard the battle, we at least have each other's arms to fall into and find love and comfort. A husband and wife who are really in love can handle any hardness trying to chase them down, and it chases after all of us at different times. When we're in love, hardness is split apart and diffused as each one absorbs the heat for the other, making the eggs of life soft and over easy rather than hard boiled. Even the ultimate hardness, the death of our sweetheart, cowers and sleeks away and never will be victorious over those who are madly and forever in love. After all, they will have learned how to stay together and keep kissing, worlds without end.

Enhancement I

My daughter works in a doctor's office and at times brings me the latest issues of medical magazines and health research. While much of it is good and worthwhile, there are still a few things where those who are supposed to know it all, really know nothing. I am sorry for my bluntness here, but when it comes to pornography there are some PhDs who are dangerous.

I always wanted to have a PhD and wish I had paid the price to get one earlier in my life. I did obtain sixty graduate hours past my MA degree, but I found myself too busy being a husband and father of nine children and serving in other capacities rather than pursue the old sheepskin. At least that is the excuse I use, lame as it may be. But I do claim a certain amount of intelligence and just because the letters PhD are next to someone's name on an article or book cover, it doesn't make it true. As in any other endeavor there are good experts and bad ones.

The latest scientific article I read about pornography and quoting three PhDs says that only 5% of porn users have a problem that interferes with daily life. The fact is that anybody who has ever looked at pornography can never claim it didn't interfere with their daily life. These PhDs say it is just, "a novelty, a turn on," for men, and women and wives need not worry about it. They even advise married couples to watch pornography together.

With misguided experts such as these advising us, little wonder the entire world is becoming pornographic. Just look at the majority of movies, TV programs, advertisements, magazines, porn sites, all of which are available now at the touch of a finger. The F word strikes our ear drums daily and seems to be common language even in the highest echelons of our elected government leaders as we continue to claim to be a nation under God. I am sure the great God of us all never uses that word. Men and women lounging in bathtubs outside in the forest or the desert as the sun goes down are promised they can be ready at any time but to call a doctor if they are still ready after four hours. What do our four-year-olds think and ask and wonder about, young and innocent as they are?

Everyone is entitled to their opinions, but some educated people lack a lot of education. The reason I know this is because of my personal experience along with a growing cadre of scientific evidence linking pornography to the addictive sickness of our society, and by good ole common sense.

In the last twelve years of my life I have personally worked and counseled with nearly 1000 individuals, mostly men, who either had in the past or were currently struggling with pornography. I will use the number 933, just to have an exact reference. Of those 933 individuals, every single one of them was unhappy, tearful, and anguish-filled. Some had become hard-core porn addicts, more hooked than those on hard narcotics. Many of them involved marriages and families, all of which were suffering with pain and sorrow because of it. Of the 933, all were unhappy, compounded by those around them who were negatively affected. Never once did I see anyone happy because of pornography. Not once.

I see marriages and families exploding, never to love again, because a husband is into pornography. The overwhelming stat of 933 out of 933 people on pornography being miserable or blowing apart beautiful wives and husbands and families is irrefutable testimony.

Enter into this discussion a little common sense. Husbands, how would we feel if every time we looked through our wife's magazines, they were filled with bare-skinned men in sensual poses and some wearing no clothes at all? How would we feel if every time she was on the computer she was looking at such images? How would we feel if she would rather spend her time with them than with us? How would we feel if we knew she was receiving more pleasure from those pictures than from our ability to make love? How could we go on? We could not, nor can she.

The facts from any reputable research are that porn is poison. It pollutes the soul and perverts the body. Porn putrifies everything it touches. It is like a potion that pours over us as a pathetic plague of perversion and any other negative words that start with the letter "P." Do not let it squeeze into your life. It is a killer of the "darkest dye."

It will destroy your marriage. All husbands and wives should take great joy in rising above this strangling sleaze of the world by having each other be the focus of their own sexuality. That is the way God intended it to be.

Enhancement J

Contrary to Karl Marx's godless statement that, "religion is the opiate of the people," I believe firmly that religion should play an important part in our life, especially our married one. There are many books on marriage one can purchase that have a religious slant and emphasis, and some of them are very good. However, with the exception of a few general references to God and a scripture or two, I have chosen to write this little book from a principle-based foundation instead of religious, for a few reasons.

First, I am interested in all marriages, regardless of their religious affiliation or belief in God. It is from marriage of a man and a woman that almost everything in this world comes, either good or bad. I have acquaintances with some who have little belief in God and religion, yet they do believe in family and its import in basic society. They are in love, they try and teach their children properly, and they appear happy. I have seen other marriages steeped in religion of one kind or another where there is no love, affection, or happiness.

I believe strongly that every marriage and family, regardless of culture, can follow certain principles, solve the problems that come, and have a joyous and happy experience together in marriage. Matrimony was made to be happy and warm and I believe happy marriages really are worth fighting for.

Second, this book is not meant to win you to God or some particular belief in him. Again, there are many written for this purpose and some of them are very good. The purpose of this little book is simply to help marriages be happy and more in love. I am convinced that if husbands and wives are continually in love, so many of the problems of the world will melt away like a snowball on the hot August runway of the Phoenix International Airport.

If children could grow up seeing their parents in love and kissing rather than angry and cursing, most would choose the love and kissing part, and this world could be a happier place to live for each generation. It all begins with marriage.

And third, I believe in St. Valentine, who in the third century led a revolt against the Roman Empire in the name of love for his precious Licinia, and for all others who seek the hallowed ground of husband and wife. Everyone should know the origin of Valentine's Day.

(Should you desire to learn more of the Valentine of whom this day of love is celebrated, I invite you to read Sidney Kuhn's historical and delightful little novel, *The Holiday Kids and The Legend of Saint Valentine* at Amazon. com)